Now in a large house there are not only gold and silver vessels, but also vessels of wood and of earthenware, and some to honor and some to dishonor.

2 Timothy 2:20

About the Cover

God made every woman to be a golden vessel of honor, decked with brilliant jewels for all the world to see.

God's Goldprint for Your Life:

The Authentic Woman of God

Discovering Your True Identity

Dorrine Jones

THE AUTHENTIC WOMAN OF GOD
©Copyright 2013 by Dorrine Jones

No part of this book publication may be used in whole or in part in any form by any electronic, mechanical or other means now known or hereafter invented, including electronic, mechanical, photocopy and recording, or in any other information storage or retrieval system or transmission by any other means, except brief quotations in printed reviews, without the written permission from the author Dorrine Jones.

Unless otherwise noted, all Scripture quotations are from the King James Version of the Bible.

Scriptures taken from THE AMPLIFIED BIBLE, OLD TESTAMENT, (AMP) Copyright ©1965, 1987 by the Zondervan Corporation. THE AMPLIFIED NEW TESTAMENT (AMP) Copyright © 1958, 1987 by The Lockman Foundation. Used by permission.

Scripture quotations taken from THE NEW AMERICAN STANDARD BIBLE®, (NAS) Copyright © 1960, 1962, 1963, 1968, 1971, 1972, 1973, 1975, 1977, 1995 by The Lockman Foundation, Used by permission. (www.Lockman.org)

Scripture quotations taken from THE MESSAGE (MSG) by Eugene H. Peterson Copyright © 1993, 1994, 1995, 1996, 2000, 2001, 2002 Used by Permission of NavPress, All Rights Reserved. www.navpress.com (1-800-366-7788).

Cover design by Katherine Field
Technical Assistance John Waldeyer

Printed in United States of America

Copyright © 2013 Dorrine Jones
All rights reserved.
ISBN 13: **978-1484953624**
ISBN 10: **1484953622**

Acknowledgements

First of all, I want it to be publicly known how much I acknowledge and honor my heavenly Father, Who is responsible for my being on the earth. I acknowledge Him as my total source of life and my reason for living. He is the Lover of my soul and my desire is to please Him all the days of my life.

Secondly, I want to acknowledge all the powerful men and women whom God has brought into my life to help bring forth my authenticity.
Among them are my husband Harry,
My former Pastor Bob Yandian,
Apostle Joyce Scott,
Prophet Cynthia Thompson,
Apostle Bheki and Prophet Shari Gamedze,
S. Renee,
Marilyn Hickey,
Myles Munroe,
Dr. Stacia Pierce,
Rhema Bible Training Center
(and the late Kenneth E. Hagin),
Kingdom University and Dr. Cindy Trimm,
Bishop Michael Pitts, and
Apostle Devin and Pastor Cordi Park

Thirdly, I want to acknowledge those who have been obedient to my heavenly Father to assist me to write this book.

Special thanks to my personal assistant and editor Donna Waldeyer, and to Katherine Field for her creativity and expertise.

INTRODUCTION

You can never become who you really are until you discover who you really are.

You can never apprehend all that belongs to you until you comprehend what you were made for. In other words, you were designed by God, the Master Designer, for greatness – to rule and reign in the earth. God wanted you here on purpose for His purpose. You are not an accident, but a distinguishing handiwork, created to exemplify God's Glory in the earth.

Until you discover how awesome He made you to be, you can never celebrate and honor the awesomeness of who God, your Father, is. He is your Source, the Responsible One who has given you His name to be used like a key to unlock your provision in this world. He is the All-Sufficient One who made a decision to love you no matter what! Your true identity, your authentic self, is locked up in Him and I want to give you some keys to unlock your purpose, power and potential so that you can manifest your true self in splendor and majesty – just like your Heavenly Father!

Authenticity is not conforming to your environment, upbringing, social status, race, creed or color. Authenticity is conforming to the divine blueprint of God for your life. I call it a "divine Goldprint" designed by heaven so you are equipped to reign on the earth. Your "Goldprint" consists of who you are, what you are to do, and where you are to be. As you walk in your "Goldprint", you will release a heavenly deposit (weight of gold) everywhere you go and whatever you do.

Everything turns to Gold!!! You truly become a Golden Vessel of honor, untarnished by man's opinions. The ways of this world carry no weight in your life.

If you don't know that His love for you was manifested through His Son, Jesus, as He was crucified, buried and raised from the dead, so that you could become His daughter, then right now you can experience that love by asking Him into your life.

If thou shalt confess with thy mouth the Lord Jesus and shalt believe in thine heart that God hath raised Him from the dead, thou shalt be saved. For with the heart man believeth unto righteousness; and with the mouth confession is made unto salvation.
Romans 10:9-10 (KJV)

Can you pray these words right now?
"Jesus I believe you died for me and
I need you in my life so I can truly live."
Now thank Him. Supernaturally you were taken out of death and darkness and translated into life and light. It's called the Kingdom of God, where the King has an awesome "Goldprint" for your life.
So let's discover the real you!

Foreword by Patricia Bailey-Jones
Master's Touch Ministries International

No other species of being has had their identity and purpose challenged as much as the woman God created. We are living in a time when the true identity of womanhood, from the creature's perspective, is being challenged daily.

The Authentic Woman of God offers a fresh and biblical linear perspective of God's original ideal concept of the authentic woman. This book will help you decipher your true identity. You will embark upon a new horizon of your uniqueness.

The author helps us as woman to understand that we have already been authenticated and validated by the most-high God. Not only are we his workmanship, we are a tool in the hand of the Master, His very own instrument of change. Only women have the power to redirect our home and our family.

Reading this book, you will be given a discreet orientation, with practical steps of how you can release your authority, and also how you as a woman can understand your assignment and calling.

Each chapter unveils practical and sound strategies of how you as women can transform into a vessel that knows how to reel her power and balance this and biblical submission, while simultaneously bring heaven to earth.

The author not only pens revelation that has been downloaded to imprint to each potential woman; she lives out what she pens, which is what makes her words rise off the page and make their lodging place within our hearts Because of the authentic annuity on her life, the author helps us to bear fruit that will remain.

CONTENTS

1. The Authentic Woman
2. You Are A Masterpiece
3. You Are Elegant, Excellent and Extraordinary
4. You Are Opulent and Affluent
5. You Are Crowned with Favor, Dignity and Honor
6. You Are On An Assignment
7. You Are A Woman of Purpose, Potential and Productivity
8. You Are A Creative Woman
9. You Are Unforgettable
10. You Are A Woman of Significance
11. You Bring Heaven to Earth
12. 7 Things That Hinder Your Authenticity
13. 3 Steps to Release Your Authenticity
14. You Are Unique

This Book is Dedicated to

My two Authentic Daughters
Patience Elayne Scott and Joy Kristina Jones,

and to my Authentic Sister
Tarry Burton Jennings,

and to all my spiritual daughters
here and in the nations.

**RELEASE YOUR VOICEPRINT,
YOUR HANDPRINT AND
YOUR FOOTPRINT
INTO THE EARTH
THROUGH THE POWER OF GOD!**

1

THE AUTHENTIC WOMAN

<u>Authentic.</u> 1. Being true to one's own personality, spirit or character. 2. Not false or imitation. 3. Real. 4. Actual. 5. Conforming to an original, so as to reproduce essential features.[1]

So what's an authentic woman? I dare say that since you are reading this book, there may be a few questions or a desire to learn more about this kind of woman.

The authentic "you" is the real, genuine you that was made in the mind of God. Your true being began in God and is released through His Goldprint for your life.

Every architect has a set of blueprints when building or developing a new building. Spiritually speaking, a Goldprint is a divine blueprint drawn by the Master Designer, God Himself, for your life. According to His design, you don't have to work for who you are, you just "be" who He designed you to be. You never have to try to "be" because you already "are". You don't even need any props or anything to help you "be" who you are.

---

[1] http://www.merriam-webster.com/dictionary/authentic, (c) 2012 Merriam-Webster Inc.

Because of His design, you are valuable. What makes you valuable and special is the love that God continuously gives you. God's love validates and affirms you as His very own – like a golden vessel of honor that He highly prizes and esteems.

So, basically authentic means to be true to one's own self, being genuinely "You" without struggle, effort or unnecessary outside influences. I would further define "authentic" by saying that you live your life from within, recognizing God as your source and reason for existence.

The Goldprint

He is your Source, and the One responsible for your existence. He is glorified when you yield to Him and allow His Spirit to use your voice as His voiceprint in the earth. He is also glorified when you allow Him to use your feet as His footprint whenever you move, wherever He needs you. And He is glorified when you allow Him to use your hands as His handprint to touch lives and fulfill His plans.

Have you ever wondered why you are here? Have you asked: "What's my purpose on this earth?" Or, "What am I called to do?" "Who am I anyway?" "Where do I fit?" "Where do I belong:"

Questions, questions, and more questions! Now most people don't go around asking these questions publicly, but secretly they keep coming up until you are able to give them answers. And that's what I want to do for you by helping you answer these questions and walk in your "purpose path" – so you can live a maximized lifestyle.

Every one of us has a Goldprint, a heavenly blueprint drawn by God. Ephesians 2:10 in the Amplified Version says you are His workmanship, recreated to do good works that are already planned; to walk in paths already prepared ahead of time. God has also pre-designed and pre-arranged a good life for you to live. This is the Goldprint of an authentic lifestyle.

> *For we are God's [own] handiwork (His workmanship), recreated in Christ Jesus, [born anew] that we may do those good works which God predestined (planned beforehand) for us [taking paths which He prepared ahead of time], that we should walk in them [living the good life which He prearranged and made ready for us to live].* Ephesians 2:10 (AMP)

There are three major areas of an authentic lifestyle:

Your Voice – What you must Say

Your Hands – What you must Do

Your Feet – Where you must Go

Over the (new) few chapters, I will help you discover the real you, the awesome woman that you are, that the world is waiting for. You have been given birth to help solve problems for others, to make a significant deposit in the earth, and to leave behind a legacy that proves that your life was worth living!

Let me describe to you ten golden discoveries and attributes that characterize an authentic woman.

1) She is A Designer's Original

2) She is Elegant, Excellent and Extraordinary

3) She is Opulent and Affluent

4) She is Crowned with Favor, Dignity and Honor

5) She Focuses on Her God Given Assignment

6) She Fulfills Her Purpose, Releasing Potential and Productivity

7) She is Creative: an Out of the Box Thinker

8) She is Unforgettable

9) She is a Difference Maker

10) She Walks in Power and the Anointing

Your authenticity is so unique, you are a designer original, a masterpiece. You are opulent and affluent. You are productive. You are unforgettable. You are precious. You have been sent from heaven on an assignment.

Together we are about to uncover and disclose the real woman that you were created to be. Let's begin our treasure hunt to discover the hidden riches within you.

2

DISCOVERY #1

YOU ARE A MASTERPIECE

<u>Masterpiece</u>. 1. A work done with extraordinary skill. 2. A supreme intellectual or artistic achievement…[2]

I will praise thee; for I am fearfully and wonderfully made: marvellous are thy works; and that my soul knoweth right well.
Psalm 139:14

First, an authentic woman is a masterpiece, handcrafted by God. You are an original masterpiece yourself. Nobody else has your DNA. Nobody else has your fingerprints. Nobody else has your personality or your character. No one has your fingerprint. No one has your footprint. No one has your voice. You are unique, you are exquisitely different. You are rare. And that is not a negative – it's a plus!

You want to be rare. You stand out in your own right because God created you and He formed you just like He wants you. That's why we

---

[2] http://www.merriam-webster.com/dictionary/masterpiece © 2012 Merriam-Webster Inc.

have to deal with abuse and not hide it. Because abuse hinders what God created you to be. It mars the beauty. It takes you out of who you really are. And you are special. You have to know that and believe it.

Sometimes we try to wear something just because it's in style and everybody is wearing it. But that's not the way it should be. You need to wear what accents you and what looks best on you. For example, don't put on pale pink when it makes you look anemic. My coloring is winter, and most of us winters need a little more dramatic color -- deep royal colors to release the beauty in us.

You've got to know you're a masterpiece. You're an original! God says in Psalm 139:14 you are fearfully and wonderfully made. Fearfully -- it means reverently. With reverence. God took time to make you. Now you need to take time to love you. God took time to design even your parents coming together so your genes could be the right combination. You've got the right eyes. You've got the right height. You've got the right DNA (divine nature and ability). It's all inclusive, nothing more, nothing less.

I was reading a story about Michelangelo who was a master sculptor. He was asked to make a sculpture for his town square. Right now it's in the museum in Florence, Italy. First of all he had to find the right materials to make it. The marble he used was a slab that he had literally passed by every day and not paid attention to. Someone had brought it down from the mountain, to do a work and left it before finishing. So he had it delivered to his workroom and he began to chisel and hammer. It took him two years to get a rough outline. Two years just to get it roughed out!

A lot of us are diamonds in the rough, trying to jump out of the Master's hand too early. You're trying to do something too quick. And God is chiseling you and hammering you and he's working on you. It could be through a pastor. It could be through your women's director. It could be through a mother or parent or someone on your job. But they're chiseling, they're working on you!

When he finished chiseling and hammering, it only presented a rough image. It took him another two years to sand it and polish it. Now think about that, because some of you are being chiseled, some of you are being sanded and polished. It took him two more years to do that. When a masterpiece is being developed it doesn't just happen overnight.

All of us have seen women who all of a sudden rise up. There's no such thing as an overnight success. If your rise is sudden, fall will be just as sudden. Anything God does is rooted and grounded. So you can be like the palm tree and you can stand in the midst of any storm. I've come through many storms but I'm still standing. It was the devil's plan to take me out, to cause me to fail, to cause me to lose my life and ministry. But being grounded meant I could hold on and still stand in the midst of tough times.

Everything that God is doing in your life is being used to develop you and to develop your ministry. He's trying to authenticate you. Whatever you're crying about or whatever you're going through, YOU'RE BEING AUTHENTICATED. You have to be proven. You have to be approved.

You have to be verified that you can do this.

Whenever the manufacturer tests a car they put it under high pressure. They run it at high speeds to make sure it can handle the road. So whatever pressure you're under is determining the degree that God can use you.

Back to the sculpture. Michelangelo for the next two years was sanding and polishing the statue. Finally it was ready to be unveiled. It was a statue of David. When it was unveiled, women began to weep and cry because it was so breathtaking. And people asked him, "How could you make something so awesome?" You know what his response was? He said "In every block of marble I see a statue as plain as though it stood before me...I have only to hew away the rough walls that imprison (it)." [3]

You Are Being Authenticated

Michelangelo already saw the statue in the slab. Before he started making it he saw it. All he did was take out everything that was not the statue. Hallelujah! I believe that's what God is doing as you read this book. You've been in hiding. Nobody knew you. Even though way down deep you knew that one day you'd be recognized. That's what God is doing -- He's going to take out everything that is not you, that He did not create, that He did not plan. He wants to unveil you.

God already saw your innermost parts. He

---

[3] http://thinkexist.com/quotation/in_every_block_of_marble_i_see_a_statue_as_plain/148720.html Copyright ® ThinkExist 1999-2012

already saw you in your mother's womb. He already saw you and He already knew the picture that you would be and that you would be so awesome. But it wasn't your time to be known just yet.

Remember the statue. God showed me there are so many women who have been hurt and He told me to minister to them, especially those who have been divorced. Because for some reason we don't seem to minister too much to the divorcees, and to those who have been hurt, those who have been bruised and wounded and then pushed aside. God is going to remove some things off of you. If you let Him, He's going to take off everything that's not the real you. Because He hasn't changed His mind. He has a plan and He will see that it is accomplished, and that you are authenticated!

This is what the Message Bible says in Jeremiah 29:11: "I know what I'm doing. I have it all planned out. Plans to take care of you and not abandon you. And plans to give you the future you hope for."

What are you hoping for? Are you thinking it's too late? I want you to be encouraged today. My assignment is to release you from being unknown and insignificant. To cause you to be sought after. Isaiah 62:4 from the Message Bible says,

> *No more will anyone call you Rejected, and your country will no more be called Ruined. You'll be called Hephzibah (My Delight), and your land Beulah (Married), Because*

God delights in you and your land will be like a wedding celebration.

God's word says "I know what I'm doing, I have it all planned out." So if God already has the plans, we don't need to make different plans. Instead, we need to agree with His plans. Proverbs 16:9 tells us;

> *The mind of man plans his way, But the LORD directs his steps.* (NAS)

And **Proverbs 19:21** (AMP) says,

> *Many plans are in a man's (or a woman's) mind, but it is the Lord's purposes for him that will stand.*

You can do all you want to do but only the purposes of the Lord shall stand. You better thank God some of those things that you planned didn't happen!

Remember, you are a masterpiece. An authenticated woman is a masterpiece. She is rare, unique, exquisitely different. You are the sculptured woman who is being handcrafted by God, about to be unveiled to the world.

3

DISCOVERY #2

YOU ARE ELEGANT, EXCELLENT AND EXTRAORDINARY

Elegant. 1. To be marked by elegance; of a high grade or quality. 2. Polished. 3. Rich with grace and dignity. 4. Elaborate.
Excellent. 1. Superior. 2. First class.
Extraordinary. 1. Going beyond what is usual and customary. 2. Exceptional.

An authentic woman is a woman who is elegant, excellent and extraordinary. She is a first-class woman who has established high standards for herself. She's free to express her God-given creativity by being extraordinary as she goes beyond what is usual and normal for others.

That's why you ought to look the best you can and act the best you can. Fix yourself up. God didn't make any ugly women. If ugly got on you, it's because of the cares and the problems and the stress. These are burdens that God wants you to cast on Him.

Revelation of the Diamond

A woman who knows that she is special in God's eyes and was made a masterpiece by the Master, is elegant. She is excellent. She is extraordinary. God gave me the revelation of this through the example of the diamond.

A church in New York asked me to speak at a women's meeting and their theme was about diamonds so I began to study the nature of diamonds. And I found that to really understand a diamond you have to know the Four C's: Cut, Color, Clarity and Carat weight.

Your Cut

An authenticated woman has a certain cut, a certain shape. The cut is all her own. She was designed that way by the Creator. That's why you have to love yourself. Maybe your hips might be a little bit bigger than what you want, but you better love every inch of them, ok?

So based on your shape, you always get the right outfits. It's all about how you dress. You can look good no matter what shape you are. Today we have all kinds of good things working for us. You can have anything you want. You can have hair long, short, color it, cut it, weave it, and so forth.

I liken it to how you fit in life – your distinct design that fits in the right place, with the right people, at the right time.

Your Color

We all have different colors that seem to bring out the best in us. We should always wear the colors that highlight our natural beauty.. Some of the most expensive diamonds are not just white diamonds, but they're blue or pink or yellow, etc. They are expensive. They're called rare. You're not going to find them in every place.

I liken your color to your personality and temperament. It's your personal touch that adds flavor and spice to your environment.

Your Clarity

And clarity means that the diamonds have defects and blemishes known as internal and external inclusions. Usually they are visible only with magnification. When you look down at your diamond you should be able to see all the way through. Or do you see some defects? Is your true character reflecting who you really are, or do others see an imposter?

I liken clarity to the "real you" behind the scenes, that others don't always see.

Many times we try to hide our mistakes in life by putting on "cover ups" to appear to be flawless. Being authentic means you are free from the pressure to make a false impression because Jesus' blood has covered us and makes us flawless and acceptable in His sight! So stop magnifying your flaws and learn to accept the gift that God made you to be!

> *Even as [in His love] He chose us [actually picked us out for Himself as His own] in Christ before the foundation of the world, that we should be holy (consecrated and set*

apart for Him) and blameless in His sight, even above reproach, before Him in love. Ephesians 1:4 *(AMP)*

Your Carat Weight

The price you will pay for diamonds varies according to their carat weight. Extraordinary women and authenticated women carry a lot of weight in the natural as well as the spirit realm.

Your carat weight refers to your value and weightiness as a woman of God. According to His Word, your value is "more precious than rubies". (Proverbs 31:10) What an encouragement to the woman in her high calling of wife, mother or entrepreneur. Rubies are highly treasured and prized, and are a symbol of freedom, charity, dignity and divine power. Rubies are very rare and have an exceptional hardness surpassed only by the diamond. Large rubies, in fact, may be worth more than diamonds. [4]

When my husband and I first got married he gave me a quarter-carat diamond. I was happy to get that. And then after ten years he gave me a zirconia®, not quite really a diamond, a big 3 carat zirconia®. That was my faith diamond. It was a big stone, and I had a faith picture, a picture of what I believed I would receive in the future.

---

[4] Ruby Gemstone Education: www.cwjewelers.com/stoneruby.htm

Then after 25 years he gave me a whole carat diamond and when we renewed our vows after 32 years, he gave me a 2 carat white silver diamond. And then my son who at the time was playing for the Colts football team gave me a two carat diamond also . So I now have diamonds on both hands. I believe God put diamonds in the earth especially for us, to enjoy. Diamond earrings, necklaces, bracelets and all are made for authentic women.

You can usually tell a prosperous woman. Even when she's dressed down she is not going to leave those diamonds behind. She may have on jeans or a sweatshirt but you can always tell, she's got her diamond earrings in her ears and diamond rings on her fingers. In other words, an elegant woman is classy, fine, graceful, majestic, stately, and tasteful in her "own way".

Let me tell you this, that a synthetic diamond or ruby is nearly identical in physical appearance to the natural eye, and can be confused with the genuine (authentic). But only a trained gemologist can tell the difference. So walk in your authenticity and let your true elegance and excellence be seen by those with an eye for true beauty.

The Word of God calls you a lively stone, being built into a spiritual house. (1 Peter 2:5) Check out your birthstone and its symbolism.

MONTH	STONE	SYMBOL
January	◆ Garnet	◆ Faith
February	◆ Amethyst	◆ Royalty
March	◆ Aquamarine	◆ Love
April	◆ Diamond	◆ Virtue
May	◆ Emerald	◆ Wealth
June	◆ Pearl	◆ Purity
July	◆ Ruby	◆ Passion
August	◆ Peridot	◆ Dignit
September	◆ Sapphire	◆ Loyalty
October	◆ Opal	◆ Purity
November	◆ Topaz	◆ Friendship
December	◆ Tanzanite Zircon Turquoise	◆ Strength

4

DISCOVERY #3

YOU ARE OPULENT AND AFFLUENT

<u>Opulent.</u> 1. Rich. 2. To have abundance. 3. Possessing great wealth.
<u>Affluent</u> 1. Generously supplied with money, property and possessions.

An authentic woman is a woman who is opulent and affluent, and one who understands her value. When God truly authenticates us He adds wealth to us. So you've got to know that more is coming to you than what you have right now. An authentic woman is a wealthy woman.

When you are affluent, you are generously supplied so that you can be a blessing. In Genesis 12:2 God tells us:

> *I will make of you a great nation, and I will bless you [with abundant increase of favors] and make your name famous and distinguished, and you will be a blessing [dispensing good to others].* (AMP)

And in Genesis 17:2 He says,

> *I will make My covenant (solemn pledge) between Me and you and will multiply you exceedingly.*

That's what He told Abraham and we are the seed of Abraham. So He wants us to be wealthy women. But we must remember that authentication comes as a process. God tells us, "If you're faithful over a few, I can put much in your hands." In other words, because you are so affluent and so opulent, you can be a big giver. Authentic women are not stingy. Also, they are tithers. They give their tenth and they give offerings.

Blessed To Be A Blessing

Before you were born, God already prepared everything you would need to do what He called you to do. Prosperity is having enough resources to fulfill your assignment.

The word prosperity in the Hebrew is *Shalom*. *Shalom* can be described with words such as peaceful, well, happy and healthy. True prosperity is based on the fact that whatever God calls for, He provides for. There will always be provision for the vision and your assignment. You should not be worrying about how you are going to make it in life, but rather understanding that provision is built into your purpose and assignment. Your opulence (abundance, great wealth) comes to remove worry from our lives.

According to Ephesians 1:3, God has already blessed you with everything you need in heavenly places in the Spirit realm. As you release faith, you make a withdrawal from the unseen realm into the seen and cause the invisible to become visible. God does not want you to depend on your own ability but His ability. He is Jehovah Jireh our provider.

Let them shout for joy, and be glad, that favour my righteous cause: yea, let them say continually, Let the LORD be magnified, which hath pleasure in the prosperity of his servant. Psalm 35:27

There is no shortage in heaven and there should be no shortage or lack in your life either.

Therefore do not worry and be anxious, saying, What are we going to have to eat? or, What are we going to have to drink? or, What are we going to have to wear? Matthew 6:31

But seek (aim at and strive after) first of all His kingdom and His righteousness (His way of doing and being right), and then all these things taken together will be given you besides. Matthew 6:33

Living to Give

One night I went to the grocery store to get a few things. And there was a little girl following her Mom and her Mom was looking at cards and I could tell that the Mom had had a hard day. And the little girl was picking up a book and saying, "Mommy, Mommy can I have it? Can I have it?" And her Mom said, "No". And the little girl had this sad face. And she didn't talk back so I could tell she was a really nice girl.

But the Lord began to deal with my heart and He said, "Buy that for her." And my response was, "You know Lord, I've got to go down this other aisle here," but I soon relented and said, "Ok let me see if I can find her." I found them on the way through the checkout, so I got right behind them and I said to the mother, "Do you mind if I buy this Bible for your daughter?" She looked at me like I was crazy. I said, "I see your little daughter wants it and it's the word of God." The little girl was saying "yes?" and the mother agreed, so I paid for it and gave her the change from a $20 bill. Then I said to the girl, "You promise me you're going to read it?" And she said, "uh hum." And the Lord said go ahead and give her $5. And by this time the mother's attitude was changing and her countenance was bright.

And then I thought about something. God was dealing with me and I thought, "How would I like to have some desires and someone comes along behind me and makes it happen?" Glory to God! That's what happens when you're opulent and affluent. You're not worried about prices and you don't say to yourself, 'That's all I got". You're not counting your pennies. You have plenty to give.

I am progressively gaining financial wealth. I have more this year than I had last year because we're working under biblical principles. If you're going to be authentic you have to be willing to give when God asks you to do so. Be willing no matter what it costs you. After that, I prayed for the mother, and I let her know, "The Lord told me to tell you that all of your needs are taken care of." Walking in your authenticity will cause divine connections, like this one, to open up along your path.

5

DISCOVERY #4

YOU ARE CROWNED WITH FAVOR, DIGNITY AND HONOR

<u>Favor</u>. 1. The divine influence upon the heart and its reflection in life; including gratitude, acceptance, benefits, gifts, grace, joy, liberality, pleasure and thanks(worthy).[5]

An authentic woman is a woman who is crowned with favor, dignity and honor. That's when you know you're authenticated -- when you're walking in favor with God and man.

Favor

The favor of God is when God uses someone to exercise their ability and their power on your behalf. To be favored means:

1) To have people go out of their way to help you.

2) To have approval.

3) To have popularity.

4) To receive preferential treatment.

---

[5]Vine's Complete Expository Dictionary of Old and New Testament Words By: W.E. Vine, Merrill F. Unger, William White Jr. *Thomas Nelson, 1996*

5) To receive special privileges.

6) To receive gracious and kind acts.

7) To receive partiality.

The Bible said of Esther, that she obtained favor from all those that looked upon her. You know, that should be your confession: "Everyone who looks at me, favors me. People go out of their way to help me. Doors that were once closed are open because of the favor of God on my life."

In Psalms 5:12, it says

He blesses the righteous with favor and compasses them about as with a shield.

The favor of God on your life will keep your enemies from triumphing over you. When you're authenticated, you have to go places and do things, so you need to have the favor of God on your life. And some people are not going to like that. They'll think, "Who do you think you are?"

Your answer? "I'm authenticated from heaven. I have a right. This is my birthright." You have a legal right to walk in favor and in the abundance of grace. This is part of your inheritance accomplished when Jesus died for you.

Ruth Chapter 2 talks about how Ruth received favor from a wealthy man named Boaz. Because of the favor of God, she became one of the richest women in the whole town because she married the man who had everything. And we know she came from Moab, lost her husband, lived with her mother-in-law who was also a widow, and traveled to a strange land.

God already knew what he wanted to do with Ruth. God had it all planned out. God wants you to be dignified, too. The Book of Proverbs, Chapter 31, talks about the virtuous woman having dignity and honor.

> *Strength and dignity are her clothing and her position is strong and secure; she rejoices over the future [the latter day or time to come, knowing that she and her family are in readiness for it]!* Proverbs 31:25 (AMP)

Dignity. 1. Quality or state of being worthy, honored or esteemed. 2. Legal title of nobility or honor. 3. Of or relating to class, rank, fashion, quality or standing.[6]

You have been crowned with dignity and honor!

> *(The Lord) Who redeems your life from the pit and corruption, Who <u>beautifies, dignifies, and crowns you</u> with loving-kindness and tender mercy...* Psalm 103:4 (AMP)

The Honor Principle

Honor causes life to flow. To honor someone means to recognize and receive from the gift God has placed in them as valuable and precious.

---

[6] http://www.merriam-webster.com/dictionary/dignity(c) 2012 Merriam-Webster Inc.

The opposite of honor is to dishonor by not showing respect or value and to treat as common or ordinary. Nothing is more distasteful to a woman then to be dishonored. You were made to be accepted, loved and highly esteemed. Reject anything less than the honor bestowed on you by God. A woman who is dishonored lacks love and becomes bitter and hateful.

> *I find more bitter than death the woman who is a snare, whose heart is a trap and whose hands are chains.*   *Ecclesiastes 7:26a (NIV)*

As you serve and honor God, He honors you as His prized possession set apart for holy use.

> *...if any man serve me him will my father honor.*   *John 12:26b*

Honor also causes you to be highly favored and esteemed by man. Psalm 5:12

Because of who you are in Christ, you have been redeemed from destruction and crowned as a queen in God's sight. You have been given royal status as a dignitary in this earth because you are God's representative. So act like you know!

6

DISCOVERY #5

YOU ARE ON AN ASSIGNMENT

<u>My Definition of Assignment.</u> 1. A divine work order with specific anointing, provision and protection that you are to release in a specific people group, place or time. 2. Anything God has called you to do to solve problems for others. 3. Your assigned sphere of authority in the earth realm where you have legal right to operate.

An authentic woman is a woman who focuses on her God-given assignment. That's the only reason why you are here – you are on an assignment.

The authentic woman must focus. In other words she is not busy doing everything. You need to learn to know that when you have been authenticated, it's not a choice, it's not an option, it's a God-given command. When you start doing your assignment you become good at it. Find out what you are good at and do it a whole lot.

So ask yourself, "What am I good at?" Then begin to do it. Your authenticity must be developed once your purpose for being is understood. For example, if you plan to open up a hair salon, make your salon different. A place with services offered nowhere else. You become a valuable commodity, and that causes you to be in demand and sought after.

Think about it. What's your value? How much do you think you are worth? Have you put a price on what you bring to the earth? Are you underestimating your value?

Some of us are broke because we do not use the creativity God has given us. He has given us specific things that will bless others in the earth realm. We have to learn that there are things that God wants to do through us.

Each of us has a God-given assignment. Proverbs 22:29 says:

See a man diligent in his business, that man shall stand before kings.

God says just be diligent; have painstaking application, earnestness and focus. Sometimes we start too many things. We want to be a jack of all trades. I want you to practice saying "No".

Learn to say "No" to those things that are not in line with your purpose, and know that you don't have to give an explanation, just a smile. Now say "No" one more time, followed by a smile. It's easier when you know what to say "Yes" to. Beware of distractions! Guard your heart and your mind if you are going to fulfill your assignment.

Jesus said it like this: I'm busy about My father's business. Do you realize that the only reason you are on this earth is to take care of kingdom business? Why are you so busy doing everyone else's business and the kingdom is lacking? You are an authenticated woman. You have a legal right to be here. You have a birthright, a certificate, a passport. You have an assignment from God.

Second Peter1:10 says be diligent to make your calling and election sure. Make it sure. That means to make that thing established and affirmed; to ratify and make steadfast.

There's no need for me to act like other people. People tell me all the time, "You remind me of so and so". I tell them, "That's good, you've got a glimpse of where God wants to take me. But I'm not them." You can learn from certain people but remember: they do not have the same assignment that you have. So I have to make my calling and election sure. That's why I can't copy someone else. I need to be genuine. Real. Authentic.

In order to do that, I have to stay focused on who God made me to be, and the assignment that He designed for me. I can't be comparing myself with others, or trying to be like others. There is no one else like me. I once heard a minister say, "God won't help you be somebody else, but He will help you to be everything that He made you to be!"

Authentic women refuse to be distracted. Right now I have one thing on my mind and that's Kingdom business. And all my friends are in Kingdom business. I'm not hanging around with anybody who's not going in the same direction.

That's why you have got to learn to detox. Detox anybody who is trying to stop you from fulfilling your assignment. Eliminate them. Get them out of your life because they will stop you. You have to have people who celebrate you and what God has called you to do.

One of my confessions is that the people around me celebrate me and they will encourage me to do what God has called me to do. You'll always know when someone is really for you, because they will encourage you to do what God has called you to do. When people want you to do what they want, that's called control. We are to be controlled only by the Holy Spirit and the love of God. Beware of controllers and manipulators who try to intimidate you through fear. Know and recognize those God is sending into your life to help you fulfill your assignment.

Two Important Things You Need to Know

- ❖ Know who has been assigned to you to help you maximize your life.

- ❖ Know who you have been assigned to help maximize their life.

DISCOVERY #6

YOU ARE A WOMAN OF PURPOSE, POTENTIAL & PRODUCTIVITY

Purpose. 1. the reason for which something exists. 2. the original intention of a thing. 3. an intended result, end or aim. 4. goal.[7]

> *Let your eyes look right on [with fixed purpose] and let your gaze be straight before you.* Proverbs 4:25 (AMP)

An authentic woman is a woman of purpose, potential and productivity. We are created by God in His image and likeness. He is eternal, and what He has placed in us will take an eternity to live out. But you were born at this time, with a purpose and mission based on this time.

Purpose tells you why you're here. Proverbs 29:18 says:
> *Where there is no vision the people perish and run wild without restraint.* (AMP)

You need a vision. You need to know the job you were made to do on earth, the people you are called to help, the problem you were designed to solve. You can only find out that vision by asking the One who made you.

---

[7] Personal Growth and Development Workbook, © 2012 Dorrine Jones Ministries, p. 6.

Psalm 39: 4 says, "Make me to know my end..." In other words, make me to know my purpose; make me to know why I'm here. This is a prayer asking God to show us what is His plan for our lives. "Why did You make me, Lord?" Psalm 39:4 continues, "...And the measure of my days, what it is that I may know how frail I am." As talented and anointed as you may be you're still not anointed for everybody and everything. Don't let people push you into something just because you're good at it. Maybe you're good at administering and they're trying to get you into the ministry of helps or think you should open a beauty salon. Is that God's plan, or someone else's?

Potential

Potential. 1. Existing in possibility. 2. Capable of development into actuality.[8]

Your potential is who you really are that has not yet come forth and what you can do that you haven't done yet. It's the power of God on the inside of you that enables you to fulfill your vision and dreams.

> Now to Him Who, by (in consequence of) the [action of His] power that is at work within us, is able to [carry out His purpose and] do superabundantly, far over and above all that we [dare] ask or think [infinitely beyond our highest prayers, desires, thoughts, hopes, or dreams]—
> Ephesians 3:20

---

[8] http://www.merriam-webster.com/dictionary/potential (c) 2012 Merriam-Webster Inc.

God's power at work in you causes your imagination to go into your future, and get previews of "coming attractions". God has promised to do beyond what we can imagine and think. WOW! Exceedingly, abundantly, beyond what you ask or think. Our imagination is not big enough to handle all that our heavenly Father wants to do for us. That is why our voice print is so important because we must release into the atmosphere what the Holy Spirit speaks to our hearts. Your mouth creates what God wants to do in the earth.

... for out of the abundance of the heart the mouth speaketh. Matthew 12:34b

For by thy words thou shalt be justified, and by thy words thou shalt be condemned. Matthew 12:37

Your voice releases life and blessing.

Death and life are in the power of the tongue: and they that love it shall eat the fruit thereof. Proverb 18:21

Do you understand what is the measure of your days? In other words, what is your potential? Your potential is your ability. It's hidden ability. It's power on reserve. It's things you have not yet done, places you have not yet gone, people you have not yet met. It's that which is still yet to come. It's the dormant ability in you to be powerful. You have the potential to be a powerful woman of God as you fulfill your mission in life.

There is a team of people already assigned by God to help you develop to your fullest potential. Did you realize God has given you your own "Dream Team"? Your Dream Team includes parents, teachers, pastors, mentors, or friends who impact your life during a particular season or period of time.

For proper growth to take place, you must be around the right people (your Dream Team) and in the right environment. The atmosphere around you will multiply what's in you and directly affect your performance and development. Something is always growing in you on a daily basis, either a weakness or a strength. Your environment affects the weakness that grows or the strength that grows.

Growth is not instant, but is governed by time. The ingredients for your growth were released from God into you when you were born. You came into the earth packaged for success!

Productivity

<u>Productivity</u>. 1. Having the quality or power of producing, especially in abundance. 2. Yielding results, benefits or profits. [9]

An authentic woman is a woman of productivity. She's able to reproduce after her kind. If God called you to sing then you ought to sing well. If He really called you to sing then you ought to be making an album and you should reproduce that album and that album ought to hit the charts and go all the way around the world. God told us in the very beginning,

> *And God blessed them, and God said unto them, Be fruitful, and multiply, and replenish the earth, and subdue it: and have dominion over the fish of the sea,*

---

[9] http://www.merriam-webster.com/dictionary/productivity (c) 2012 Merriam-Webster Inc.

and over the fowl of the air, and over every living thing that moveth upon the earth.   Genesis 1:28

So you ought to dominate in whatever area God called you to do.

If you're not dominating it could be that you're not doing the right things, the things God planned for you to do, because He put a dominator on the inside of every one of us.

When God spoke that blessing in Genesis 1:28, He set in motion what I call the Four Laws of Productivity. God told the first humans to be fruitful, multiply, replenish and subdue.

The Law of Fruitfulness means to grow from within, to increase the talents, abilities and potential you were created with. Authentic women are fruitful. They bring their seeds of greatness to maturity, producing a perpetual harvest.

The Law of Multiplication means there will be exponential growth and progress. Authentic women multiply. They increase and reproduce after their kind.

The Law of Replenishment means restoration, Swealth, luxury and extravagance. Authentic women replenish. They refill, renew, and spread throughout the earth what God has deposited within them.

The Law of Subduement means to master and overcome oppositions and fears. Authentic women subdue. They conquer, manage and bring order.

These four laws lead to dominion. Dominion means to rule, control, master and take authority over. Authentic women are called by God to dominate in the earth over the forces of hell. Get alone with God and find out what His plan is for your life, and start doing it. You'll see that productivity will come forth when you're doing what God called you to do because you were designed to bear fruit in every season of your life.

8

DISCOVERY #7

YOU ARE CREATIVE

Creative. 1. Having the quality of something created rather than imitated. 2. Clever, innovative or imaginative.[10]

An authentic woman is a woman of creativity. She thinks and acts "outside the box". That means that what she does is extraordinary. Get out of the box! I know you probably have been in a church service when you got out of the box, did something unusual, and you got back in because of the pressure and the comfortability. That's called conforming to the norm!

When you're doing things you never done before, you can feel very frightened. You have to do some things you've never done before, but it's ok. Because it's in you to be creative. You were created in God's image. You were created for expression!

Also, you don't know just how much is in you until you begin to step out. And then you'll begin to see the power of God that will flow through you. When you are

---

[10] http://www.merriam-webster.com/dictionary/creative (c) 2012 Merriam-Webster Inc.

flowing in God's power, the things that will come out of your mouth will scare you. Then you'll ask yourself, "Is that me?"

I learned this from a very well-known minister who said, "When you're heart is in the right place and you love God and you desire to please Him, He's obligated to cause the right people to come into your path. He's obligated to get the right knowledge to you that you need to know." Is your heart right before God? Do you desire to please Him? Then God is obligated help you.

You know what God has been dealing with me about? God says, "Ask Me". "You have not because you ask not". He said "Ask me for creative ideas. Ask Me for something creative. Every day ask Me for a creative idea."

You've got to ask God. He said "Ask and you shall receive." Remember, all of heaven is backing you up and angels are waiting on your command.

You are not alone. We shouldn't act like we are here as aliens all by ourselves, trying to make our own life, struggling with kids, struggling because we are trying to solve our own problems. Ask and then listen when the Holy Spirit gives you new ideas, new paths, new ways to solve your problems.

Be creative. Think outside the box. Job 33:4 says

> [It is] the Spirit of God that made me [which has stirred me up], and the breath of the Almighty that gives me life [which inspires me]. (AMP)

The creativity will come through God stirring you up. That's why you can't afford to be sad. You can't afford to have down days or be depressed. When you're depressed you can't hear the voice of God. When you don't have joy you hinder His voice and you can't hear what God is saying for you to do.

That's why you have to rejoice. Rejoice!

We are told in Paul's letter to the Philippians (4:4) *"Rejoice in the Lord always, and again I say, Rejoice."* I already know that God has put something on the inside of me that has the ability to cause women to be motivated. To cause them to see who they are. To cause blinders to fall off their eyes. So when I come into a place I come in to change the atmosphere. I come in to set the captives free. Glory to God! And you can do the same. It's a decision to choose to be happy and enjoy life!

Isaiah 61:1-2 says:

> *The Spirit of God, the Master, is on me because God anointed me. He sent me to preach good news to the poor, heal the heartbroken, to announce freedom to all captives, pardon all prisoners. God sent me to announce the year of his grace — a celebration of God's destruction of our enemies—* *(The Message)*

Wow! A celebration of God's destruction of our enemies! God will fight for you! Replace all your fears with rejoicing and release your creativity! Starting today ask the Holy Spirit to give you a creative thought for your home, as a mother, as a wife, on your job, or in the ministry. This is the time to walk in your creativity.

REMEMBER WHO YOU ARE!

1. *A Designer's Original*
2. *Elegant, Excellent and Extraordinary*
3. *Opulent and Affluent*
4. *Crowned with Favor, Dignity and Honor*
5. *Focused on Your God-Given Assignment*
6. *Full of Purpose, Potential and Productivity*
7. *Creative: an Out of the Box Thinker*
8. *Unforgettable*
9. *A Difference Maker*
10. *Walking in Power and the Anointing*

9

DISCOVERY #8

YOU ARE UNFORGETTABLE

<u>My Definition of Unforgettable</u>. 1. Making an impact that leaves a mark to be remembered.

As an authentic woman, you move and act according to the voice on the inside of you that is responsible for your being. This kind of woman responds out of a deep sense of necessity and gratitude all mixed in one.

A good example of this is the woman who came and sat at Jesus' feet. (Luke 7:40-50) This woman was led to pour expensive oil on His head as an act of true worship and submission. According to the Bible, there is no mention of her having honors or awards as a woman of renown. Her name isn't even mentioned, or any facts given except that the oil was very costly, the equivalent of a year's wages.

However, when you walk in your authenticity, what appears as a waste or as unnecessary can be the very thing that separates you from the crowd and puts you in the spotlight. You see, you don't have to ask anybody's permission to do what you are led to do by the Spirit of God.

This was the woman's time to be known for the gift she possessed in the natural – an alabaster box. When she broke the box, the fragrance was unstoppable. Everyone in the room could smell it. Her act got the attention of the heavyweights in the room. All eyes were on her as she bowed down and wept, causing her tears to fall upon Jesus' feet. Wow! What an unforgettable scene that must have been!

Did the disciples praise her and thank her? No. They were indignant, saying *"To what purpose is this waste? For this ointment might have been sold for much, and given to the poor." Matthew 26:8-9*

This woman was walking in her unique self and Jesus validated her by saying, "*Why berate her for doing such a good thing to me?*" *Matthew 26:10 (NLT)* In other words, "Don't try to make her fit into your mold. Don't disturb the DNA that I placed within her. She is on assignment and she is fulfilling her purpose!"

You must understand that you are called to release the precious ointment on the inside of you. You are called to minister to the Body of Christ and to those you are assigned to in the world.

This woman's act of worship is an example of being "in the timing of the Lord". She was anointing Jesus' body for burial. No one else in the room knew that at the time, but that was the significance of her act and why she was willing to pour out such costly service on Him. When you move in authenticity, you have the future in view. You are not led by day-to-day crises.

Jesus declared over this woman,

> *She has done what she could; she came beforehand to anoint My body for the*

burial. And surely I tell you, wherever the good news (the Gospel) is proclaimed in the entire world, what she has done will be told in memory of her. Mark 14:8-9 *(AMP)*

What the disciples saw as a waste, insignificant and disgusting, Jesus saw as significant, even necessary to fulfill prophecy. As you move in your authenticity according to the leading of the Holy Spirit, Jesus will defend you. When your enemies rise up against the real you, they will fall back and be ashamed. God tells us, "*Vengeance is mine. I will repay.*" (Romans 12:19)

What kind of legacy, or memorial, will you leave behind? How do you want to be remembered? Begin by developing a personal image statement based on your purpose and assignment.

Do you have in your mind a picture of your personal legacy? If not, let me share with you my personal image statement so that you can understand how to develop your own:

"I am a woman of excellence, influence and style, called by God to set the captives free. While maintaining a level of royalty, dignity and distinction, I impact the lives of those I come in contact with by releasing God's power and His Presence." [11]

Your legacy should match your God-ordained purpose. God wants you to be remembered!

As you develop your own legacy statement, consider the following questions:

---

[11] School of the Woman Training Manual, Module 6, Dorrine Jones Ministries © 2008

1. Who am I?
2. What is God's plan for me?
3. What are my dreams?
4. What do I want people to see when I arrive?
5. What message do I want to convey?
6. What kind of differences do I make in the lives of people?
7. What kind of impact would you like to leave on your family, community and the world?

There is no one like you. You don't have any competition except in your own mind. You were designed to make and leave an unforgettable mark!

10

DISCOVERY #9

YOU ARE A WOMAN OF SIGNIFICANCE

<u>Significance</u>. 1. Having meaning, influence or effect. 2. The quality of being important.

An authentic woman's significance is in her point of difference. It's not how similar you are to others. It's your difference. There is a point of difference and that is your distinguishing mark. That is your label. That's what sets you apart. That's what makes you more than just another woman.

Now if you don't know what your point of difference is, you need to find out. It can be seen in your style. It can be seen in your dress. It can be seen in your intellect. The way your carry yourself. The way you walk. The way you handle business. There is a distinction. And you need to move in that distinction because that's where your significance is. And it will make you rich.

The Bible says in Esther 2:15, when Esther's turn came she obtained favor in the sight of all of them. That means all the other women. There were a whole lot of women there, but Esther had the favor of the King and all the other women, because of her authenticity.

There are a whole lot of women in our lives. But only you have been given your assignment. Only you have been authenticated for this assignment, and that's what you have to recognize and value.

Do you know how different you are from others? Or do you try to copy someone else because you are uncomfortable being yourself? When others talk about you, what do they say? How do people see you? Do they see you as different or in your difference?

And remember that Esther found favor with the others "when her turn came". Not before. Wait for your turn. By waiting you allow God to prepare the way. He has already prepared you for your assignment, and because He is Sovereign, He is planning the way you should go. So being impatient and rushing ahead of His plan can only cause you delay or setbacks.

Think of yourself as a photograph being developed. It takes time. Believe that you were created to be beautiful, excellent, prosperous, always increasing. That's God's plan for you. He designed your purpose before He even made the world.

How you see yourself will change. As you receive God's image of you, you will be changed "from glory to glory" and your excellence, beauty and significance will also be changed.

Enjoy your differences, and remember that you were made to be different and unique.

11

DISCOVERY #10

YOU BRING HEAVEN TO EARTH

An authentic woman is a channel of anointing and power from God to the earth. Authentic women release power from the throne room.

How to Bring Heaven to Earth

You have been authorized and deputized as God's representative on earth to establish His Kingdom, to change the culture and mindsets so they look and act just like heaven. You have the power to be a change agent and transform your environment so it becomes like heaven on earth.

Thy kingdom come, Thy will be done in earth, as it is in heaven. Matthew 6:10

An authentic woman spends time with God and receives power. That's where she's authenticated. You're not authenticated to do what God has called you to do unless you're spending daily time with God. The reason some people are drying up and envious and jealous is because there's no Presence of God in their lives. You have to renew yourself.

> *But they that wait upon the Lord shall renew... They shall mount up with wings like an eagle.*   Isaiah 40:31

In my book, THE EAGLEFIED WOMAN, I wrote a chapter called, "Learning to Fly". In it I write about spending time in God's presence and how we are changed:

"In His Presence, we are continually transformed into the image of God's Son, and we can act more and more like Him. According to Isaiah 40:31, as we wait we are changed from strength to strength, faith to faith, and glory to glory. As we are changed, we exchange all those things that hinder us and block our relationship with the Lord.

"Paul tells us how this happens in his 2 Corinthians, chapter 3 verse 18:

> *And all of us, as with unveiled face, [because we] continued to behold [in the Word of God] as in a mirror the glory of the Lord, are constantly being transfigured into His very own image in ever increasing splendor and from one degree of glory to another; [for this comes] from the Lord [Who is] the Spirit.*   (AMP)

"But we don't always see results instantly. These changes come to "those who wait". "Psalm 139:23-24 tells us:

> *Search me, O God, and know my heart: try me, and know my thoughts: And see if there be any wicked way in me, and lead me in the way everlasting.*

[handwritten: a MIRROR / Do you see what I see - Says God. / I see —]

By asking His Spirit to search our spirit, we can discover and confess anything that will get in the way of our fellowship with Him.

"By learning about the Lord, we develop a longing to be with Him, a hunger and thirst that can be satisfied only by His Presence. The Psalmist says, 'O taste and see that the Lord is good!'. As with food, no one can taste for you. There is no explaining what something tastes like. Only you can experience and know for yourself just how satisfying God's Presence can be."[12]

It is in God's Presence that you will learn your true identity. As you commune with Him, He will authenticate you. Anything authentic has been confirmed. It has been validated, certified, bona fide, justified and testified of... I'm talking about you... someone who has already been warranted, sanctioned and authorized to operate in the earth realm.

We need to have validation, in the spirit as well as in the natural. For example, I have a passport. My passport gives me the legal right to travel in and out of the country. By the way, if you're going to be an authenticated woman you've got to get a passport. You can't be serious about God and not have a passport.

My passport is recognized. It's been validated. It's been confirmed. It proves who I am, because it even comes with a picture of me. If we have a passport in the natural, it's because there's a spiritual passport which you and I have already been issued when we joined God's family.

And I heard the Spirit of the Lord say a picture of you has been taken. As you discover who you are, and

---

[12] The Eaglefied Woman, by Dorrine Jones, pg. 32-36, 2011

accept God's validation and recognition, an angelic photograph is being taken of you and it's being placed down in hell to let the devil know that no demon from hell can stop what God has called you to do. As an authentic woman, demons need to know who you are.

Spiritual Passport

My spiritual passport is based on the promises in God's covenant with believers, and He has already decreed that all my needs will be met. (Philippians 4:19)

In my US passport, it says here, "The Secretary of State of the United States of America hereby requests all who it may concern to permit the citizen national of the United States named herein to pass without delay." As it relates to me spiritually, that means, I can do it. I can pass without delay or hindrances. That's why we have got to learn how to overcome and bypass every resistance.

One time when I was on my way to an engagement to minister, we got turned around while driving and I thought we were going in the opposite direction. We had to figure out which way to go to reach our appointment. We were able to overcome in spite of circumstances by walking in our authority. We were equipped to call the shots because we had been authenticated by God. HalleluJah!

My passport also says, "…Any hindrance, and in the case of need to give all lawful aid and protection." That means everything I need in order to obey God has already been released for me. I don't have to worry about money. I don't have to worry about help, equipment, offices, people. It's already been released. All I have to do is use my faith and tap in and make the withdrawal by calling those things that are not to show up. I cause them to show up. Because it's already been given.

It also means I have protection. I have angels on assignment to protect me and to keep me safe as I obey God. Just because you can't see them, doesn't mean they don't exist!

Matthew 6:10 tells us to pray the Kingdom of God come, His will be done. This can only happen as we walk in His power and execute the Father's will on earth as it is in heaven. In heaven there is no sickness, no stress, no lack, no pain, etc. Then there should be none on earth!

When we release healing, sickness has to go. When we cast out demons, we recover what was held captive by the enemy. We bring heaven to earth when we release God's Word and power to flow through us against sickness, disease, broken marriages, depression, poverty, lack and so forth.

7 Things That Hinder Your Authenticity

1) Comparison

2) Jealousy and Envy

3) Impatience

4) Lack of Productivity

5) Lack of Self-Esteem

6) Lack of Focus

7) Lack of Planning

12

7 THINGS THAT HINDER YOUR AUTHENTICITY

<u>Hinder.</u> 1. To hold back, delay, impede or prevent action.

You may not have noticed that there are hindrances holding you back, preventing you from accomplishing all that God has designed for you to do. Like the sculptor Michelangelo, God wants to remove those things that are not really you.

Remember that statue we talked about earlier? Michelangelo saw the finished product even as he was looking at a slab of marble. God knows the plans He has for you, good plans, and He wants to remove those things in your life that the cares of life have burdened you with.

One day as I was listening to the Lord, I said, "Now God, if we're so authentic and all of this is in our power, why aren't we manifesting it?" I began to think about my own self. Why do I struggle? Why am I going through so much? He began to give me answers in the natural and in the Spirit.

So let's examine what hinders you from becoming all you were made to be. "To hinder" means to hold back, delay, impede or prevent action. You may not have noticed that there are hindrances holding you back, preventing you from accomplishing all that God has designed for you.

Seven Hindrances

#1 Comparison

He showed me that the biggest hindrance to your walking in your authenticity is comparison.

2 Corinthians 10:12 says, *But they measuring themselves by themselves, and comparing themselves among themselves are not wise.* You're a foolish woman if you do that.

The Amplified Bible in the same verse says you are without understanding and behave unwisely. That means you lack understanding. You don't understand who you are. You don't understand how awesome you are, and what a masterpiece you are. Why would I try to copy someone when I'm an original myself?

Comparison will eat you up. It will mess you up. Some of you are looking at women that you see and you don't know what they've been through. You would never even want to trade places. You would never even be able to stand the test.

#2 Jealousy and Envy

The second thing is jealousy and envy. A very good friend of mine defined jealousy as wanting what someone else has. But envy says "I don't want what you have and I don't want you to have it either."

For example, a woman becomes very jealous over how God has blessed you with a new home and speaks against you to intimidate you or make you feel bad about your blessings. Then someone else begins to envy you and says you shouldn't have that new home. They aren't being covetous (wrongly desirous of wealth or possessions; greedy)[13]. They just don't want to see you blessed.

This attitude can also lead to a spirit of indignation which releases bitterness, anger and jealousy all wrapped up together as a destructive arrow to pierce your soul and your spirit.

In Hebrews 12:15, we are warned:

> *See to it that no one comes short of the grace of God; that no root of bitterness springing up causes trouble, and by it many be defiled...*

When you start comparing, then you start getting jealous and you become very envious and bitter. The Amplified Version says it more forcefully:

> *Exercise foresight and be on the watch to look [after one another], to see that no one falls back from and fails to secure God's grace, (His unmerited favor and spiritual blessing), in order that no root of resentment (rancor, bitterness, or hatred) shoots forth and causes trouble and bitter torment, and the many become contaminated and defiled by it..*

---

[13] http://dictionary.reference.com/browse/covetous?s=t Dictionary.com, LLC, Copyright © 2012

#3 Impatience

The third hindrance is impatience. Guess what? Your turn is coming. Your time is coming. If you are born and you are reading this book, you have a set time.

You have a *kairos*[14] moment. You need to prepare for an opportunity that does not yet exist. This is preparation time, time to get ready. James 1:4 says," *But let patience have her perfect work."* The Amplified version says,

> *Endure, but let endurance and steadfastness and patience have full play and do a thorough work, so that you may be a people that's perfectly and fully developed, with no defects, lacking in nothing.*

No defects, lacking in nothing. That's when you know you've passed the test. You've walked through some things and allowed them to authenticate you, and not push you to complain and quit.

Unless you have been prepared, you are still unable to fulfill your assignment. You need patience while the preparation is being completed.

#4 Lack of Productivity

And the fourth hindrance is non-productive activity. You need to do only those things that produce the greatest energy in your life and the things that produce the greatest results.

---

[14] a fixed and definite time, the time when things are brought to crisis, the decisive epoch waited for, the right time, limited period of time to what time brings, New Testament Greek Lexicon http://www.biblestudytools.com/search/?q=kairos&rc=LEX&rc2=&ps=10&s=References

Don't just get busy. Get focused. Look at the possibilities and compare them with your purpose. What were you made to do? Then do it.

#5 Lack of Self-Esteem

The fifth thing is low self-esteem. And I think that's a big one. My simple definition of self-esteem is loving yourself. How much do you really love yourself? Look what the Psalmist says about you in Psalm 139:14:

> *I will praise thee (O Lord); for I am fearfully and wonderfully made.*

If you don't love yourself you're saying you don't love what God made.

God esteems you, and you should too. From the same Psalm, we learn:

> *How precious also are thy thoughts unto me, O God! how great is the sum of them!*
> *(v. 17)*

Jesus said to love your neighbor as yourself. (Matthew 22:39.) His commandment includes loving yourself!

That's why your worship is so important because the more you love Him and spend time with Him, the more He reveals to you who you are. And He reveals to you what He called you to be. You then begin to realize the power that's in your life and you begin to appreciate and value what He values.

#6 Lack of Focus

And then the sixth hindrance is lack of focus. You will never maximize your potential when you are not doing the things God called you to do. It's so, so true.

God's word tells us in Proverbs 4:23-27

> *Keep thy heart with all diligence; for out of it are the issues of life ... Let thine eyes look right on, and let thine eyelids look straight before thee. Ponder the path of thy feet, and let all thy ways be established. Turn not to the right hand nor to the left: remove thy foot from evil.*

I've learned from experience not to allow distractions to break my focus and hinder my productivity. Most distractions would be considered good things. But there is an assignment. When we break our focus it prevents us from producing what God has called us to do. Most people fail because of broken focus!

#7 Lack of Planning

I'm really big on this seventh hindrance. Do you have a personal growth plan? I am surprised how many women have no plan. What do I mean by that? Luke 2:40 says that Jesus grew and became strong and He was filled with wisdom and grace. In other words there was a plan He was following.

Personal Growth Plan

A personal growth plan begins with a vision, a mission statement and goals. When you sit and think about your future, what do you see? Does what you see, your vision, match what God says about you?

Mission Statement

Do you have a mission statement that explains in writing who you are and what you will do? There's no business that you visit that doesn't have a mission statement on their walls somewhere.

Goals

What are your goals? What does God want you to be doing this very moment? Look around you and decide what responsibilities He has placed in your hands, and recognize that He has a plan for you right where you are. Write that down as your current goal. What has He called you to do long-term? Write that down as your long-term goal.

The Bible says in Psalm 20:4,

> *May He grant you according to your heart's desire and fulfill all your plans.*

But you have to have some plans to present to Him.

Action Plans

What are your action plans? Action plans describe how you will reach your goals. You can't just live from day to day and from Sunday to Sunday. Because you have been spending time with God, listening to His Spirit and reading His word, you know what God has called you to do.

Confessions

Once you know your goals, then create some action plans. Then start making confessions. You begin to say what God says about you. For example, "I am who God says I am. I will have what God says I will have. I will go where God says I will go." (See Appendix for a list of daily and weekly Confessions.)

One day I was sitting in a woman's meeting and I said, "I will speak in this church someday". That wasn't coveting or desiring something that I couldn't have. I was agreeing with what God had already showed me. And it came to pass.

When God shows us something, faith has to have corresponding action. You don't really believe it until you speak it and release it.

I produced a teaching CD describing the power in your mouth because God began to show me that words are containers that can release life or death into the atmosphere around us. You are what you say!

Something is wrong when you spend all this time in the presence of God, laying before God, saying "O God I love you Allelujah!" and then you get up and keep right on doing what you've been doing? What good is it? You've got to take what you've received from the Lord and start speaking!!!

So when God reveals something to you, agree with Him by speaking it out. When He places a desire in your heart, agree by claiming it in prayer. Then thank Him and praise Him for His power and love that will bring it to pass!

Healthy Lifestyle

Another part of the personal growth plan should deal with your health. You can't just eat everything you want. Do you really think you're going to be healthy and fulfill God's will? You need to eat healthy meals. You need to work out your menus to balance the food your body needs. You need exercise. You need proper rest. You can't stay up all night and rise early and think you're going to produce one hundred percent!

Financial Planning

Another part of your personal growth plan is financial. What are you doing with your money. How do you plan for the future? Do you have some storehouses? Storehouses are those assets that help you survive droughts, like Joseph's storehouses in Egypt. Do you have a way to handle emergencies?

Are you a tither? Do you give 10 per cent of every dollar back to God? The tithe is for your benefit, as Malachi 3:10 explains:

> *Bring your full tithe to the Temple treasury so there will be ample provisions in my Temple. Test me in this and see if I don't open up heaven itself to you and pour out blessings beyond your wildest dreams. For my part, I will defend you against marauders, protect your wheat fields and vegetable gardens against plunderers.* (MSG)

Do you give as the Holy Spirit leads you to give? Do you honor God with your giving? This is also for your benefit.

> *Honor the Lord with your capital and sufficiency [from righteous labors] and with the firstfruits of all your income; So shall your storage places be filled with plenty, and your vats shall be overflowing with new wine.* Proverbs 3:9-10 (AMP)

Do you have a savings account? If not, open one today so God can bless you as you become a good steward over what He has given you. 2 Corinthians 9:10 tells us,

> *Now he who supplies seed to the sower and bread for food will also supply and increase your store of seed and will enlarge the harvest of your righteousness.* (NIV)

The sower is the one who obediently gives to the work of the Kingdom and distributes where the Holy Spirit leads. This is the one whose seed is multiplied.

As a good steward of what God has given you, you will see that He, in turn, "shall supply all your need according to his riches in glory by Christ Jesus." (Philippians 4:19)

13

3 STEPS TO RELEASE YOUR AUTHENTICITY

Step One is Worship

Authentic women are worshippers. Worship is a lifestyle. You'll see the worship on them. They don't just serve God, they worship Him. And they don't just worship in the sanctuary. They worship with their lives, they adore Him, they love Him at home, on the job, wherever they are.

Authentic women know that they are strengthened in God's Presence. They know that

> ...*Those who wait for the Lord [who expect, look for, and hope in Him] shall change and renew their strength and power; they shall lift their wings and mount up [close to God] as eagles [mount up to the sun]; they shall run and not be weary, they shall walk and not faint or become tired."* Isaiah 40:3 (AMP)

Step Two is Prayer

Authentic women maintain continuous communion with God through prayer. Prayer is her lifestyle. Prayer releases power in you and through you. So, little prayer, little power. Without prayer, your authenticity will not come forth. It just won't. In times of prayer you learn who you really are.

And you have to choose to pray. Sometimes it's a hard choice.

> *"[Jesus] told them a parable to the effect that they ought always to pray and not to turn coward (faint, lose heart, and give up)."* Luke 18:1 (AMP)

Also, prayer is more than petitioning God for things. When you look at prayer as spending time with your Father, you learn that prayer is fellowship and communion with the Lover of your soul.

Step Three is The Word of God

The authentic woman gets into the Word of God. The Word empowers you. It enlightens you. It feeds you. Reading and listening to the Word also feeds your faith.

> *"Man shall not live and be sustained by (on) bread alone, but by every word and expression of God."* Luke 4:4 (AMP)

Jesus said *"every word"*. As Paul wrote to his disciple Timothy,

> *"Every Scripture is God-breathed (given by His inspiration) and profitable for instruction, for reproof and conviction of sin, for correction of error and discipline in obedience, [and] for training in righteousness (in holy living, in conformity to God's will in thought, purpose, and action."* 2 Timothy 3:16 (AMP)

As an authenticated woman you need to be in the

word daily. God tells us to "study to show yourself approved" – authenticated. – "a workman that need not be ashamed." (2 Timothy 2:15)

But after we have read the Word, we must be doers of the Word. James 1:22 tells us that when we are hearers of the Word only, and not doers, we deceive ourselves. The Word is profitable for reproof, correction, and training so that you,

> *...may be complete and proficient, well fitted and thoroughly equipped for every good work.* 2 Timothy 3:16 (AMP)

To accomplish our God-assignment we need the equipping of God's Word. And the more we look into the Word and do it, the more we will take on the same image and authenticity as Jesus.

But I found out something else. Not only do I need to read the Word but I need to read other books related to the assignment that God has given me. When He says renew your mind, He wasn't just talking about the Bible alone. Whatever area your assignment is in, read accordingly. Learn about those areas. Prepare yourself for success in your God-ordained assignment.

What is God's Plan?

As we are being developed in our authenticity, there are things that God wants to do. I believe I was called to help you discover your authentic self. You are just like Mary, whom we discussed in a previous chapter. She had an alabaster box, which was something precious, very precious. They say it represented about a year's wages. And she poured its contents over Jesus' head.

This is what God needs you to do. He needs you to break loose today so that what is most precious in you can come out. The real, authentic you that can make a significant mark in the earth must be released.

The Spirit of the Lord said to me, "I am raising up women who will break their alabaster box and release the thing inside them that is precious. Their authenticity on the inside of them is locked up." God says, "When they break it, they are released in it, and they will release an anointing into the earth realm that will usher in His return."

Mary prepared Him for His burial. Prophetically, we will anoint the Body of Christ with our gifting, our anointing, and with the authenticity He has put in each of us.

Are you understanding the purpose of your authenticity? Are you ready to be released from the lies and labels that others have put on you and to arise and shine because your light (the revelation of God's Goldprint for your life) has come and His Glory is about to burst forth in and through you?

> *Arise [from the depression and prostration in which circumstances have kept you—rise to a new life]! Shine (be radiant with the glory of the Lord), for your light has come, and the glory of the Lord has risen upon you!*
>
> *For behold, darkness shall cover the earth, and dense darkness [all] peoples, but the Lord shall arise upon you [O Jerusalem], and His glory shall be seen on you.*
>
> *And nations shall come to your light, and kings to the brightness of your rising.*
> *Isaiah 60:1-3 (AMP)*

14

FINALLY, YOU ARE UNIQUE

<u>My definition of Uniqueness</u>. 1. Your distinctive differences which set you apart from the ordinary and qualify you to become extraordinary.

Unique means being the only one; being without a like or equal; unequaled; unusual.

You are made in the image and likeness of God, therefore you are in the God class.

You are an original design, carefully thought out, hand-crafted by God.

You are unique, distinct and different, making you necessary and needed.

You are rare, precious and valuable.

You were born to succeed and excel in the earth.

You have the ability to be great, and to prosper at whatever you put your hands to.

You are distinctively different on purpose.

You have a unique personal style.

Your life is but a reflection of the touch of the Master Designer's Hand.

Psalm 139 gives us a behind-the-scenes look at how God formed you. Let's take a look:

> *For You did form my inward parts;*
> *You did knit me together in my mother's womb.*
>
> *I will confess and praise You for You are fearful and wonderful and for the awful wonder of my birth!*
> *Wonderful are Your works, and that my inner self knows right well.*
>
> *My frame was not hidden from You when I was being formed in secret [and] intricately and curiously wrought [as if embroidered with various colors] in the depths of the earth [a region of darkness and mystery].*
>
> *Your eyes saw my unformed substance, and in Your book all the days [of my life] were written before ever they took shape, when as yet there was none of them.*
>
> *How precious and weighty also are Your thoughts to me, O God! How vast is the sum of them!*   Psalm 139:13-17

God wants to authenticate you. As stated in the beginning, authenticate means to confirm, to justify, to validate, to warrant, to assure the certainty or validity of something or someone. But you cannot be authentic unless you have purposed in your heart that you are going to obey God. Sad to say, there are a lot of women doing their own thing. If it doesn't match God's plan, you won't walk in your true authenticity.

Jesus said "I came into this world not to do my own will but the will of Him who sent me. He that sent me is with me." He also says "I am not alone." So we're talking about God authenticating women who are in agreement with the will of God for their life.

For the authenticated woman, there is a Goldprint that has been released from heaven when you were born. You may not have it in your head. But you have it in your innermost being. The word of God gives you the legal right to operate and to carry out His will for your life.

Each of us has been created to be an original design. There is an authenticity coming forth. There is a uniqueness coming forth. There is an originality coming forth from you now that you have discovered the 10 things that reveal authenticity.

So let's discover your authentic self by truthfully answering the following questions. Don't rush. Write down the answer that you know to be true for you, not what you conformed to in the past.

1) What do you enjoy doing?

2) What causes you to feel fulfilled?

3) What are you good at?

4) What makes your life necessary and significant?

5) What sets you apart from other women?

6) What causes you to be different?

7) What is your assignment on earth?

8) What makes you so valuable?

9) What makes you unforgettable?

10) What are you doing that is unprecedented? (Fresh, unheard of, unfamiliar, unaccustomed to)

11) Describe your uniqueness!

If you are unable to answer this last question, ask God today for creative, innovative thoughts, or a "God idea". Then prepare yourself to have your imagination stretched. Hear and obey. See and do.

According to 1 Corinthians 2:9,

> ...*Eye has not seen and ear has not heard and has not entered into the heart of man, [all that] God has prepared (made and keeps ready) for those who love Him.*

These are things that the Spirit of God wants you to know about you and about your assignment.

> *Yet to us God has unveiled and revealed them by and through His Spirit,...the [Holy] Spirit Who is from God, [given to us] that we might realize and comprehend and appreciate the gifts [of divine favor and blessing so freely and lavishly] bestowed on us by God.*
> *1 Corinthians 2:10, 12*

Finally, when you receive God's Goldprint for your life, you will become a golden vessel of honor in the Master's hand. You will be used for His purposes as you establish the Kingdom:

- *LET YOUR VOICE BE HEARD AS A SILVER TRUMPET*
- *LET YOUR HANDS DO THE GREATER WORKS*
- *LET YOUR FEET GO INTO ALL THE WORLD AND MAKE DISCIPLES*

ABOUT THE AUTHOR

Dorrine Jones is the Founder and President of Dorrine Jones Ministries (formerly called "Heart to Heart Ministries"). Described as "A Ministry Designed with the Woman In Mind", its mission is to unlock the treasure within women and to release their God- given purpose and potential.

Dorrine is founder of The School of the Woman, designed for women of all cultures to discover their uniqueness and to become difference-makers. She has been developing high impact women for over 25 years, helping them to walk in their distinctiveness. Dorrine has traveled to over 30 nations, as well as various parts of the US. She has also ministered through radio and television in the US and the Caribbean and most recently she has also appeared on Trinity Broadcasting Network (TBN).

Dorrine served for ten years as president of The School of the Warrior, a two-year training course equipping men and women in spiritual warfare. She has authored several training manuals on personal development, as well as the book, *Selah Time*, with its sequel audio book with accompanying music. Her recent book, *The Eaglefied Woman*, teaches women how to soar to their highest potential.

An alumna of Kingdom University School of Ministry, conducted by Dr. Cindy Trimm, she attended Rhema Bible Training Center in Oklahoma, before joining her husband, Harry D. Jones, in pastoring Abounding Grace Family Worship Center in Media, Pennsylvania. She is listed in the National Register's Who's Who in Executives and Professionals.

Dorrine and her husband parented four children through college and post-graduate studies, and enjoy the blessing of their several grandchildren. They reside in Pennsylvania.

APPENDIX

PRAYER TO RECEIVE SALVATION

If you haven't become a part of the Kingdom of God yet, pray this prayer:

Dear Heavenly Father,
I come to you in the Name of Jesus. Your Word says "...him that cometh to me I will in no wise cast out." (John 6:37) So I know You won't cast me out, but You take me in. And I thank you for it.

You said in Your Word "... if thou shalt confess with thy mouth the Lord Jesus, and shalt believe in thine heart that God hath raised Him from the dead, THOU SHALT BE SAVED... For whosoever shall call upon the name of the Lord shall be saved." (Romans 10:9, 13a)

I believe in my heart that Jesus Christ is the Son of God. I believe He died in my place as payment for my sins, and was raised from the dead for my justification. I am calling upon His Name – the Name of Jesus – so I know, Father, that you save me now. Your Word says "...with the heart man believeth unto righteousness and with the mouth confession is made unto salvation." (Romans 10:10)

I do believe with my heart, and I confess Jesus now as my Lord.
Therefore, I am saved, and a part of Your Kingdom. Let Your will be done and Your Kingdom come in my life.

Date_____

Welcome to the Kingdom of God! Now keep close to God so He can authenticate you!

Dorrine Jones

INFILLING OF THE HOLY SPIRIT

The Holy Spirit is a person. God says he was given to us to live with us. He wants to dwell in us so that He can flow out of us to others with His gifts.
You can receive His fullness right now wherever you are. Below are scriptures to guide you as you ask the Holy Spirit to fill you.

GOD'S PROMISE
Acts 1:8

But ye shall receive power, after that the Holy Ghost is come upon you: and ye shall be witnesses unto Me both in Jerusalem, and in all Judaea, and in Samaria, and unto the uttermost part of the earth.

YOU MUST ASK IN FAITH
Luke 11:9-10, 13

And I say unto you, Ask, and it shall be given you; ..
For every one that asketh receiveth; . . .

If ye then, being evil, know how to give good gifts unto your children: how much more shall your heavenly Father give the Holy Spirit to them that ask him.

YOU MUST RECEIVE BY FAITH
Acts 2:38-39

Repent, and be baptized every one of you in the name of Jesus Christ for the remission of sins, and ye shall receive the gift of the Holy Ghost.
 For the promise is unto you, and to your children, and to all that are afar off, even as many as the LORD our God shall call.

YOU MUST OPEN YOUR MOUTH AND SPEAK
Acts 2:4

And they were all filled with the Holy Ghost, and began to speak with other tongues, as the Spirit gave them utterance.

John 7:38
He that believeth on me, as the scripture hath said, out of his belly shall flow rivers of living water.

STEPS TO BE FILLED

1. You must be born again according to the Prayer of Salvation. (Romans 10:9-10)

2. Believe by faith you are forgiven of your sins.

3. Then ask the Holy Spirit to fill you to overflowing (Luke 11:9-10, 13)

4. The manifestation will cause you to speak in a heavenly language according to Acts 2:4.

5. Now open your mouth and let the rivers of living water flow. (John 7:38)

6. Receive power to be His witness. (Acts 1:8)

NOW THAT YOU ARE FILLED BEGIN TO BUILD YOURSELF UP BY PRAYING IN THE SPIRIT

Jude 1:20 But ye, beloved, building up yourselves on your most holy faith, praying in the Holy Ghost

Weekly Affirmations for the Authentic Woman

Monday
I am accepted and loved by God Himself.

Tuesday
I am strong in the Lord and in the power of His might.

Wednesday
I am made in the image and likeness of God, therefore I speak things into existence because I have the mind of Christ.

Thursday
I am blessed to be a blessing to many.

Friday
I am God's battle axe and weapon of war.

Saturday
I am anointed with the Holy Ghost and power and I go about doing good and healing all who are oppressed of the devil because God is with me.

Sunday
I attend to God's word.
I keep it in the midst of my heart.
It is life and health to my flesh.

CONFESSIONS (Taken from Proverbs 31)

Day	I AM	Proverbs 31
1	Powerful	Verse 10
2	Invaluable	Verse 10
3	Trustworthy	Verse 11
4	Compassionate	Verse 12
5	Creative	Verse 13
6	Thrifty	Verse 14
7	Diligent	Verse 15
8	Business Minded	Verse 16
9	Strong in Body	Verse 17
10	Positive about my Endeavors	Verse 18
11	Watchful	Verse 18
12	Skillful	Verse 19
13	Charitable	Verse 20
14	Merciful	Verse 20
15	Fearless	Verse 21
16	Royally Dressed	Verse 22
17	Respected	Verse 23
18	Industrious	Verse 24
19	Dependable	Verse 25
20	Confident	Verse 25
21	Wise (discreet)	Verse 26
22	Kind	Verse 26
23	Prudent (Practical)	Verse 27
24	Energetic	Verse 27
25	Good Mother	Verse 28
26	Good Wife	Verse 28
27	Excelling in Virtue	Verse 29
28	God Fearing	Verse 30
29	Deserving	Verse 31
30	Honored by the public	Verse 31
31	Bearing much fruit	Verse 31

School of the Woman — The Finishing Touch

**Learn How to Become Your PERSONAL BEST
Break Your Glass Ceiling DISCOVER YOUR AUTHENTICITY
And UNLOCK YOUR POTENTIAL**

Many women who have not known their God given purpose have become victims of abuse - whether emotional, physical or sexual. From the Garden of Eden until now women have come under satanic attack.

God has raised up *School of the Woman* in answer to the cries of women throughout the nations. With all the advances in technology and education today, the need of developing virtuous women still remains unmet. *School of the Woman* is a finishing school designed with God's woman in mind. A high impact curriculum has been developed to train, instruct and bring to maturity the essence in every woman.

School of the Woman is ordained by God to cause every woman to:

1. Come into a greater perception of who she is
2. Understand the will of God for her life
3. Exceed, excel and expand
4. Be profitable and prosperous in life
5. Unmask her true identity

School of the Woman Curriculum:

Module 1	Personal Growth and Development
Module 2	Spiritual Growth and Development
Module 3	Financial Growth and Development
Module 4	Physical Fitness Development
Module 5	Social Growth and Development
Module 6	Image Profile and Development

For more information visit www.dorrinejonesministries.org

Additional copies of this book may be purchased at
www.Amazon.com

For more information about Dorrine Jones, see
www.dorrinejonesministries.org

Made in the USA
Charleston, SC
23 March 2014